Reza

VALI

Persian Folk Songs
(Set No. 16C)
for Bassoon and Piano

Transcribed by
Darius Farhoumand

Piano Score

Duration ca 20'

KEISER®

Persian Folk Songs (Set No. 16C)

By

Reza Vali

Persian Folk Songs (Set No. 16C) is the sixteenth set of an ongoing cycle of Persian folk songs that I have been composing since 1978. The piece was written for Kian Soltani and consists of seven songs some of which are based on authentic Persian folk melodies and some are composed in the style of a folk song (imaginary folk songs). Here are brief descriptions of each song:

Songs No. 1, Longing: The lover is longing for a reunion with the beloved.

Song No. 2, In Memory of a Lost Beloved: This is a dialogue, across the dimensions, between the deceased beloved and the grieving lover. The song reflects upon the grief of separation-- in this case, separation by death.

Song No. 3, The Girl from Shiraz, The sensual and the spiritual aspects of love intersect in song No. 3. The text of the original folk song "The Girl from Shiraz" is highly sensual. The melody of the third song is accompanied by quotes from the Christmas carol *Silent Night*, and Wagner's *Tristan and Isolde.*

Song No. 4, Love Drunk (mastom-mastom): this is a well-known folk song from Shiraz. The original text of the song describes the intoxicating joy when the lovers meet.

Song No. 5, In the Style of an Armenian Folk Song. This is an imaginary folk song written in the style of an Armenian folk song. The song reflects the melancholic aura of some of the Armenian-Iranian folk music. There is a large minority of Armenian-Iranians who live in Iran. They are an inseparable part of the Iranian culture and I love their music.

Song No. 6, Imaginary Folk Song: this song is written in the style of a folk song (imaginary folk song). It is an up-beat scherzando.

Song No. 7, Folk Song from Khorasân: This song is a folk dance from the northeastern province of Khorâsân. This is a raucous song containing fast tempi, up-beat rhythms, rapid change of the harmony, and loud dynamics.

Acknowledgements from the Arranger

I would like to extend my sincerest thanks to

Reza Vali,
for your beautiful music as well as your willingness to collaborate and support making it accessible for bassoonists.

Ronald Krentzman,
for your essential copyist contributions and for creating the newly engraved edition.

Rémy Taghavi,
for collaborating with me on this project and bringing attention to the practical aspects of bassoon performance.

Janna Baty,
for providing me with the texts and translations to the original set, *The Being of Love.*

Yale School of Music,
for giving me the opportunity to present and premiere this music on stage in Morse Recital Hall, Sprague Memorial Hall at Yale University in March 2025.

Sandro Alexander Tsereteli,
for your exceptional talents as a pianist and your dear friendship.

Frank Morelli,
for the outstanding guidance you have given to my studies, the artistic insights with which you have musically empowered me, and the care and to which you have encouraged my growth.

My Grandmother,
who, at the age of 90, has looked after me throughout my journey, and for whom I dedicate much of my professional work.

My Parents,
for unconditionally loving my ideas, my idiosyncrasies, and my innocence.

Persian Folk Songs (Set No.16C)

Arranged by Darius Farhoumand

REZA VALI

I.

12
molto rit.
Tempo I ♩= 112
rit.
ff
mf
molto rit.
Tempo I ♩= 112
rit.
mf
mp
p
(Ped.)
15
B Piu mosso ♩= 138
(start slowly and gradually speed up)
più anim. poco a poco
rit.
f
mp
Ped.
19
a tempo
più animato
sostenuto
f sub.
p
(Ped.)

molto rit.
Adagio ♩ = 40
22
ff
sfz
molto rit.
Adagio ♩ = 40
f
sfz
(Ped.)
Eb - F# trill fingering: from LH 12, RH 123; trill LH 1, RH 23
24
(ff)
sfz
ff
pp
(Ped.)
27
poco più animato
ff
p
poco più animato
(Ped.)
29
BSN.
rit.
f
p sub.

stringendo poco a poco
cresc.
Adagio subito ♩ = 40
ff
sffz
pp
C Lento ♩ = 96
rit.
a tempo
mp molto espressivo
p soft, like an echo
f sub.
p espressivo
mp
Ped.
ff sfz
f
pp
pp sub.
fp
(Ped.)

Page intentionally left blank to facilitate page turn

II.

D
Lento ♩. = 72
ff
sf
Ped.
3
Meno mosso ♩. = 60
f
Meno mosso ♩. = 60
ppp sub. sempre sim.
(Ped.)
5
(Ped.)
8
(Ped.)

10
ff
(Ped.)
13
(Ped.)
15
rit. _ _ _ a tempo
ff
rit. _ _ a tempo
pp sub.
ff
sf
(Ped.)
18
E
f
ppp sub.
(Ped.)

20
(Ped.)
22
mf
f
(Ped.)
25
(Ped.)
28
F
ff
F
(Ped.)

30
poco sostenuto
poco sostenuto
(Ped.)
32
a tempo
f
a tempo
pp
(Ped.)
35
rit.
G Più mosso ♩. = 96
ff
pp
rit.
G Più mosso ♩. = 96
ff
sf
(Ped.)
38
G.P.
Adagio ♩ = 40
f
rit.
8va
sf
sfz
Adagio ♩ = 40
rit.
G.P.
(Ped.)

Più mosso ♩= 92
Meno mosso ♩= 82
rit.
Meno mosso ♩= 69
Largo ♪= 50
♩=56
♩=42
Meno mosso ♪= 44
Ped.
(Ped.)

III.

H Adagio ♩= 42
H Adagio ♩= 42
p
l.v.
Ped. sempre (leave the sustaining pedal down throughout this movement)
5
mf molto espressivo e cantabile
mp
pp sub.
8

10
ppp
13
mf
l.v.
15
start slowly and gradually speed up
I
f
rit.
mp

17
a tempo
poco sost.
a tempo
poco sost.
19
a tempo
a tempo
21
mf
(♩. = 42)
(♩. = 42)

23
15ma
ppp
25
(♩=42)
(15)
15ma
(ppp)
f
27
J
p
mf
mp

*) Stay motionless for five seconds, then attacca to the next movement.

IV.

K
Allegro scherzando ♩= 138
ff
sfz
ca. 3"
Ped.
5
with flair and "schmaltz" like a folk musician
f espr.
p sub.
pp
(Ped.)
9
ff
f
pp sub.
13
ff sfz
mf
p sub.

16
mf cresc.
pp
(Ped.)
19
cresc.
(Ped.)
poco rit.
a tempo
23
f
ff sfz
poco rit.
a tempo
ff
poco rit.
a tempo
ff sfz
poco rit.
a tempo
sfz
ff
(Ped.)

rit.
L a tempo
rit.
L a tempo
p sub.
pp sub.

38
ff sfz
sfz
sfz
mf
ff
sfz
sfz
sfz
sfz
Ped.
41
M
mf cresc.
M
pp
p
(Ped.)
44
cresc.
(Ped.)
48
ff sfz
ff
ff
sfz
ff
(Ped.)

50
F♯ multiphonic
(underblow)
ca. 2"
sfz pp
ff
sfz
sfz
ca. 2"
pp
ff
Ped.
Molto meno mosso ♩= 69
rit.
molto rit.
54
sfz pp sub.
3
5
pp
8va
ff
sfz
ppp
l.v.
Ped.
Subito più mosso ♩= 126
molto rit.
57
fff
ffff sfz
sfz
8ba

Page intentionally left blank to facilitate page turn

V.

N Andante ♩. = 58
mf molto espressivo
N Andante ♩. = 58
mp molto espressivo
Ped.
5
♪ = ♪
sfz p
(Ped.)
Ped.
9
mf
mp sub. molto espressivo
(Ped.)

13
rit.
O Poco più animato ♩. = 66
p
f sub.
mf sub.
(Ped.)
17
sostenuto
Meno mosso ♩. = 50
rit. poco a poco
♩. = ♩ (♩=50)
21
Molto meno mosso ♩ = 44
rit.
3
mp
mf
p

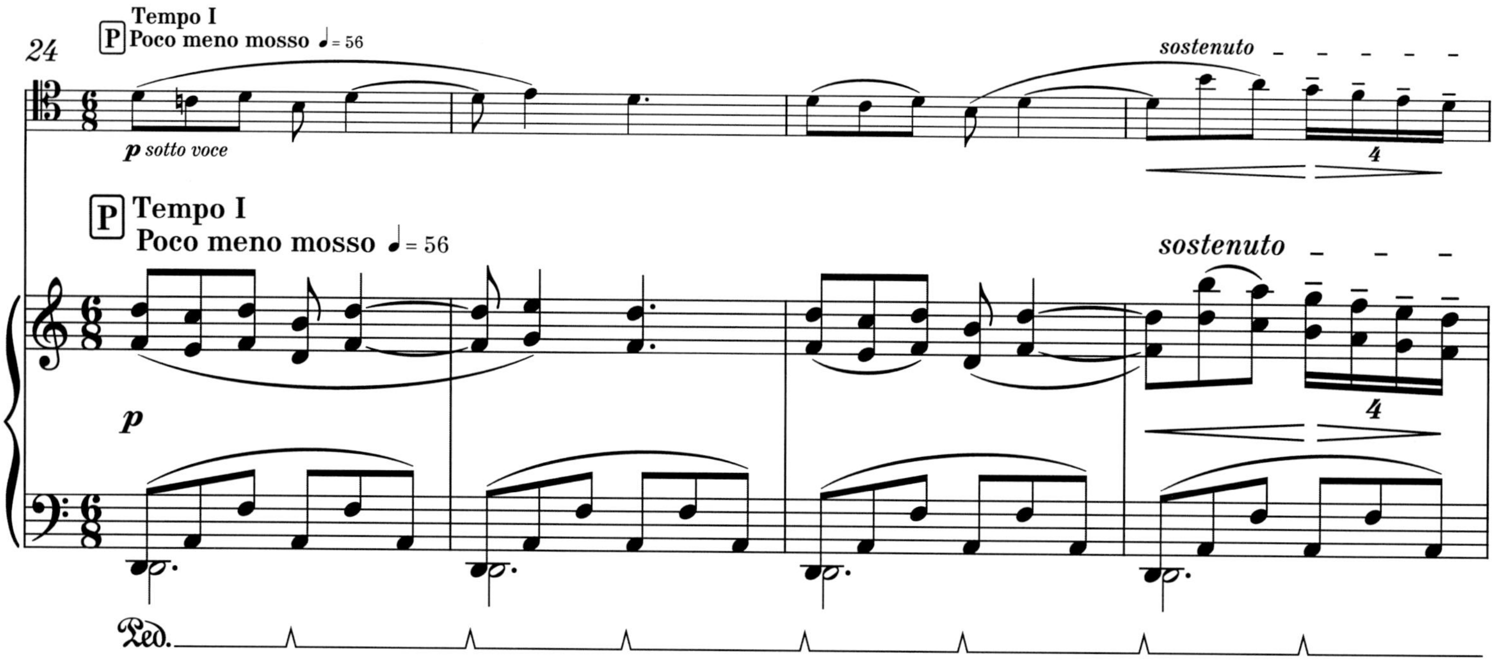
24
Tempo I
Poco meno mosso ♩= 56
p sotto voce
sostenuto
Tempo I
Poco meno mosso ♩= 56
p
sostenuto
Ped.

28
rit.
Meno mosso ♩. = 44
poco rit.
poco fp
pp
rit.
Meno mosso ♩. = 44
poco rit.
(Ped.)

VI.

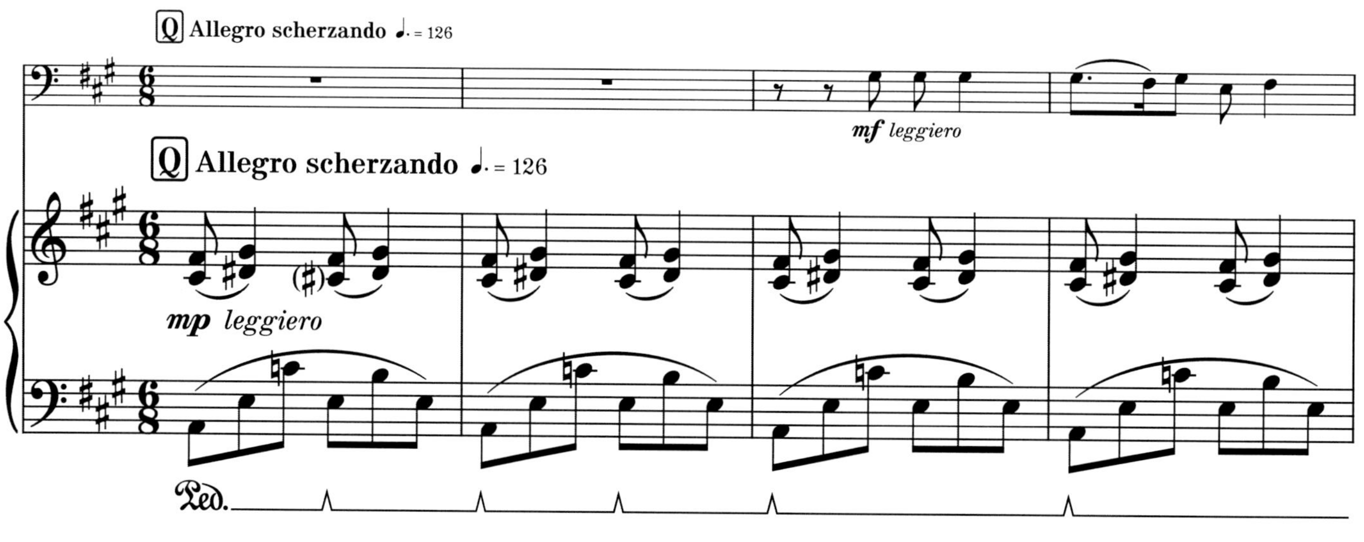
Allegro scherzando ♩. = 126
mf leggiero
Allegro scherzando ♩. = 126
mp leggiero
Ped.

5
mf
mf
(Ped.)
9
rit.
mf
rit.
(Ped.)
13
Poco meno mosso ♩. = 120
f
Poco meno mosso ♩. = 120
mf
Ped.
17
molto rit.
molto rit.
(Ped.)

21
R Molto meno mosso ♩. = 50
poco sost.
a tempo
sostenuto
f molto espressivo
ff
come forward
mf
f
(Ped.)
25
molto rit.
più molto rit.
Adagio ♩ = 48
30
Poco più mosso ♩ = 50
mp
rit.
p
34
stringendo poco a poco
S Tempo I
Allegro scherzando ♩. = 126
sfz
pp
f
mp leggiero
Ped.

38
mf leggiero
mf
(Ped.)
42
mf
mf
(Ped.)
ossia
molto rit.
46
molto rit.
3
3
7:4
cresc.
f
(Ped.)

49
Tempo I ♩. = 126
mf
Tempo I ♩. = 126
mp
(Ped.)
53
(Ped.)
57
dim.
pp
ppp
(Ped.)
61 T
T
8va
Solo
like a bird
8va
Ped. sempre

64
(8)
67
pp
rit.
sfz
15ma
69
Meno mosso ♩= 60
rit.
mp
p
ppp
l.v.
attacca

VII.

U Molto allegro ♩= 132
ff sfz
U Molto allegro ♩= 132
ff sfz
♪ = ♪
8va
Ped.
sfz

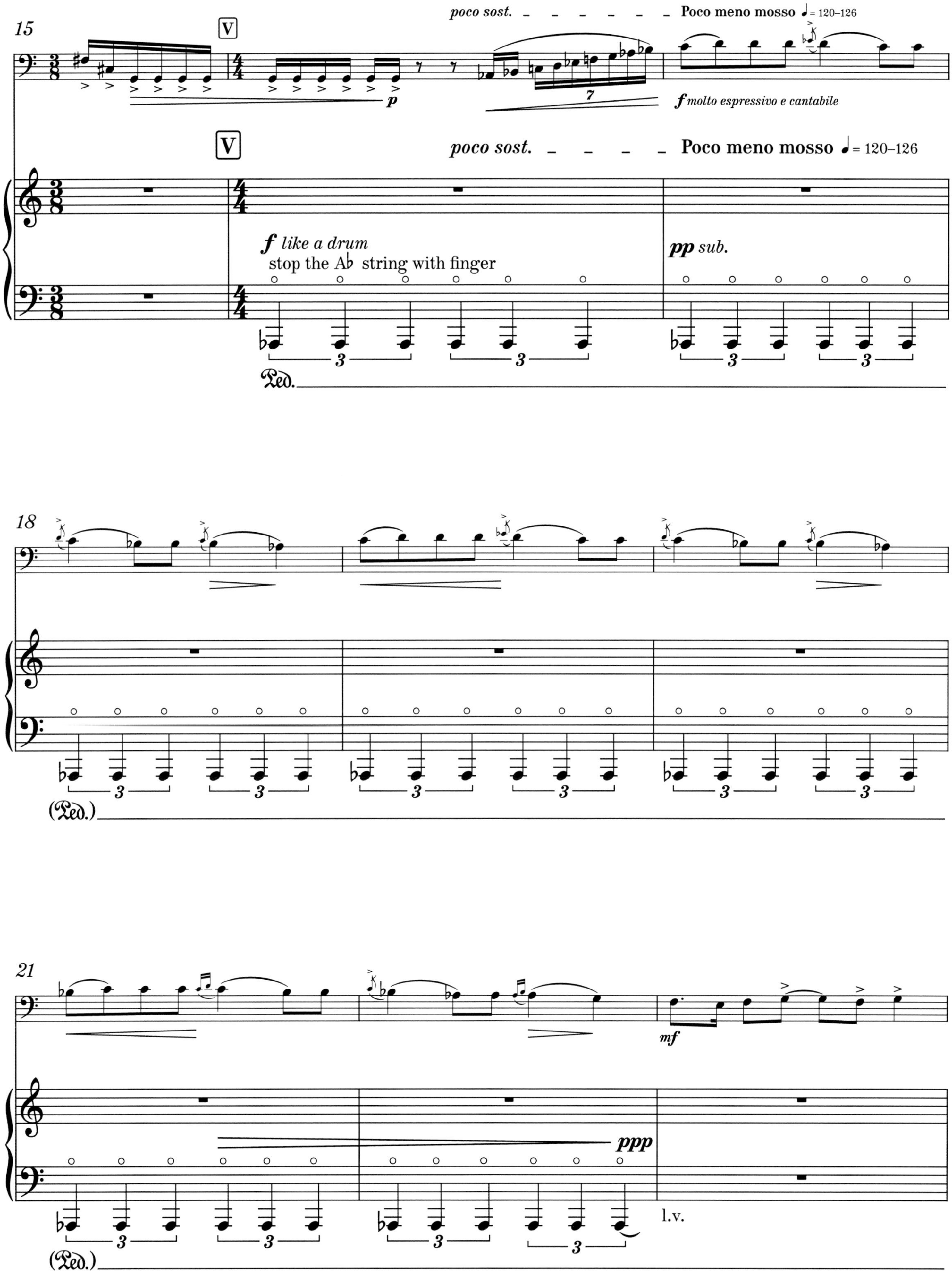
15
V
poco sost.
Poco meno mosso ♩= 120–126
p
7
f molto espressivo e cantabile
V
poco sost.
Poco meno mosso ♩= 120–126
f like a drum
stop the A♭ string with finger
pp sub.
3
Ped.
18
(Ped.)
21
ppp
mf
l.v.
(Ped.)

24
f
pp sub.
f sub.
ff
(Ped.)
Ped.
27
fff
cresc.
31
W
sfz
fff sfz
Ped.

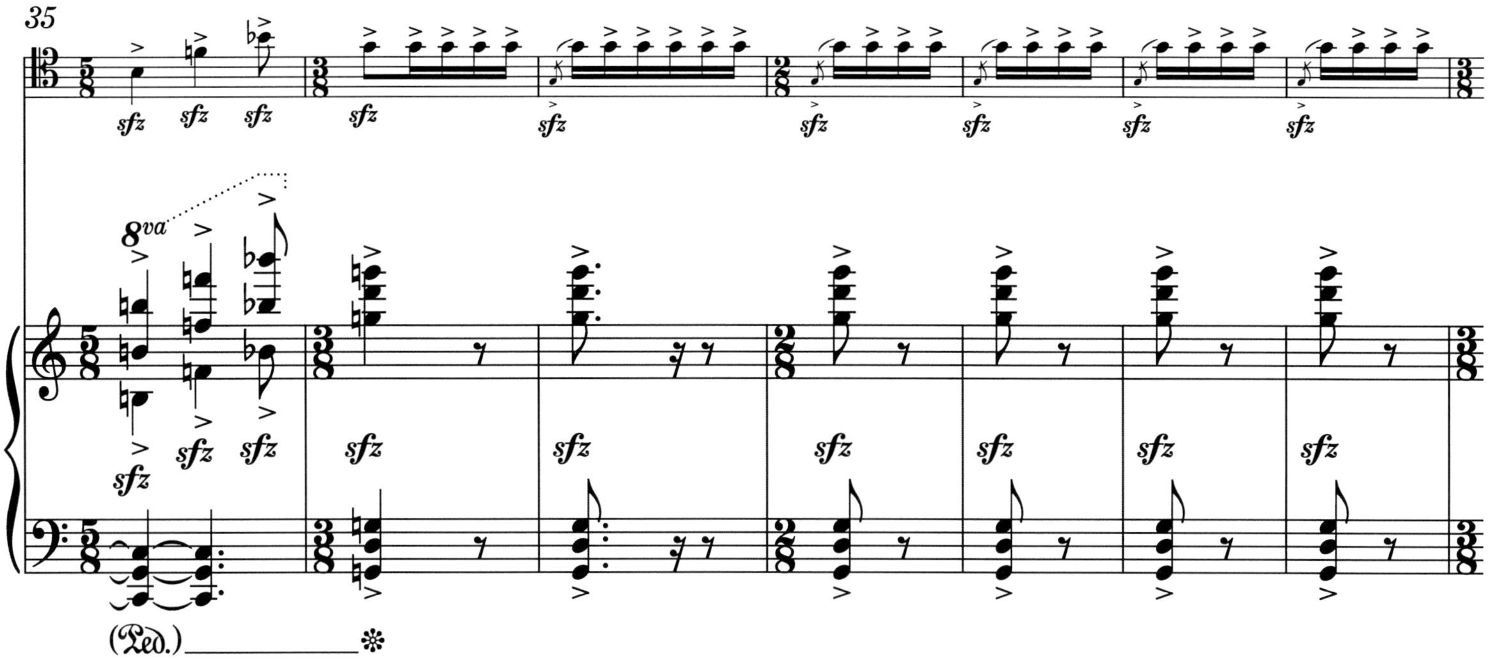
35
8va
sfz
(Ped.)

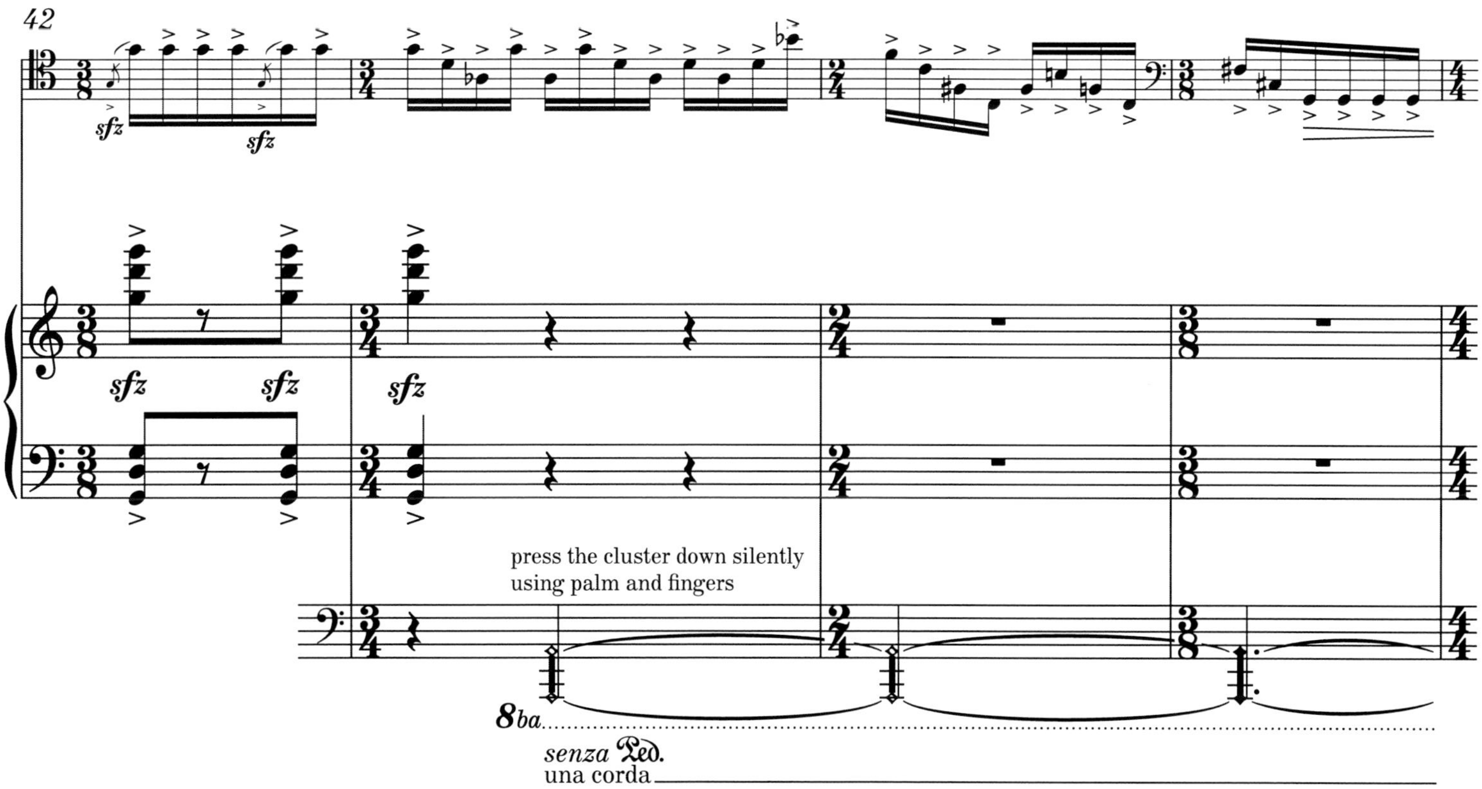
42
sfz
press the cluster down silently
using palm and fingers
8ba
senza Ped.
una corda

*) This may be played one octave lower through measure 58.

51
(8)
(u.c.)
53
mf sub.
l.v.
f

56
pp sub.
f sub.
ff
Ped.
58
p sub.
Y
Meno mosso ♩ = 110
cresc. poco a poco
pp
come forward
61
(Ped.)

63
ff
sfz
ff
(Ped.)
Ped.
65
pp sub.
pp sub.
(Ped.)
67
(Ped.)

69
ff
(Ped.)
71
fff
Z Più mosso (Tempo I) ♩= 132
Z Più mosso (Tempo I) ♩= 132
sfz
74
f sub.
f sub.
(Ped.)

*) Underlying rhythm of the piano part.

83
(Ped.)
85
fff
sfz
sfz
sfz
sfz
sfz
sfz
8va
(Ped.)

Più mosso ♩= 144
BB
bisbigliando
RH
B♭
G
A♭
sempre simile
sfz
tr
fff
ppp sub.
fff sub.
BB Più mosso ♩= 144
8va
8ba
(Ped.)
ppp
Ped.

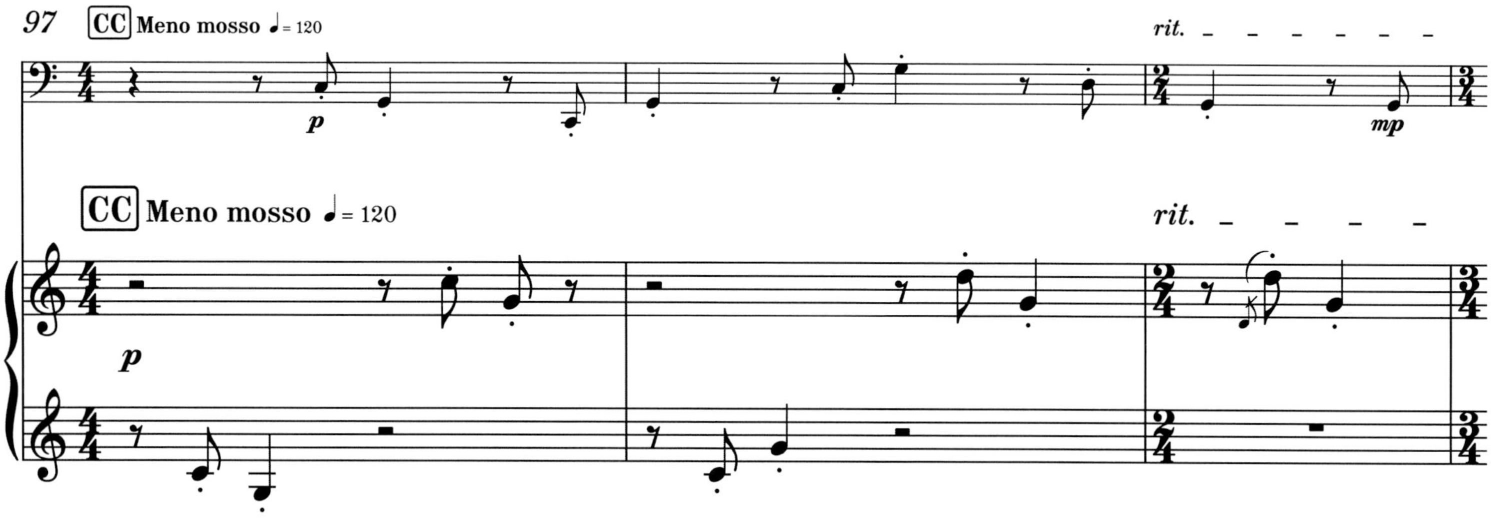
97
CC Meno mosso ♩= 120
rit.
p
mp
CC Meno mosso ♩= 120
rit.
p

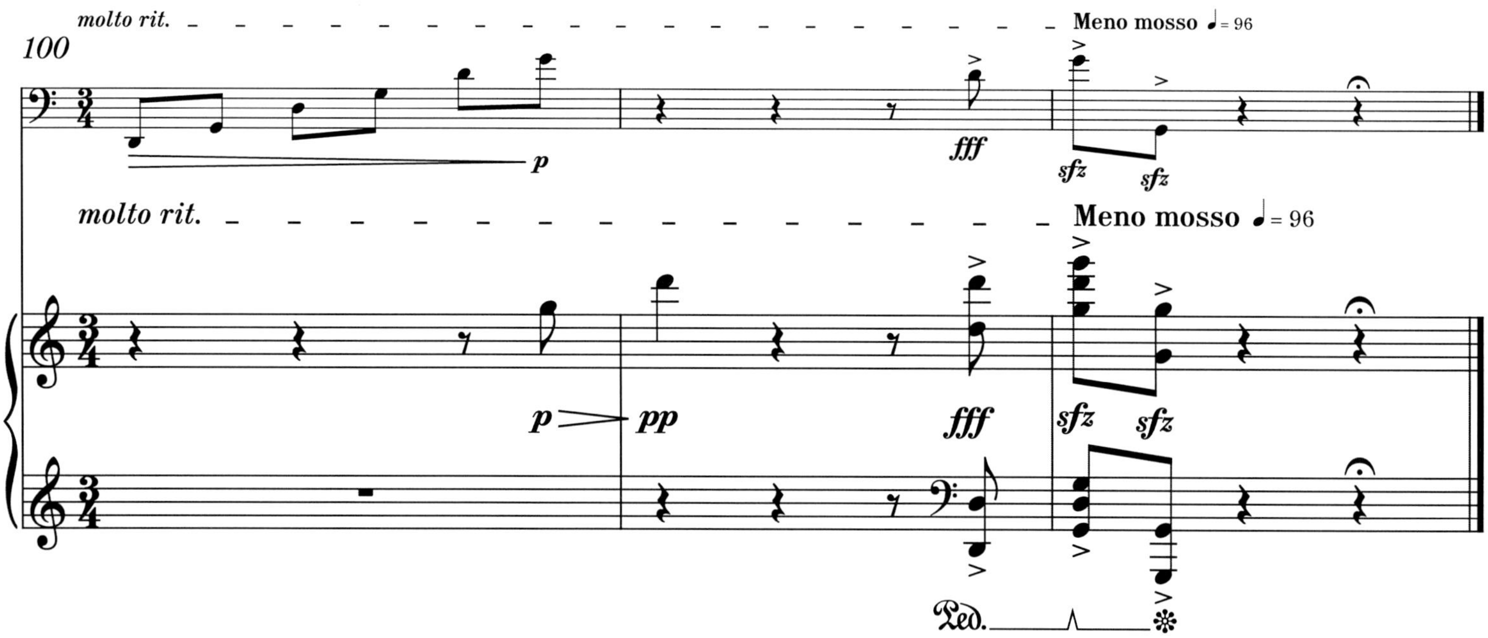
molto rit.
100
Meno mosso ♩= 96
p
fff
sfz
sfz
molto rit.
Meno mosso ♩= 96
p
pp
fff
sfz
sfz
Ped.

Bassoon

Persian Folk Songs (Set No.16C)

Arranged by Darius Farhoumand

REZA VALI

I.

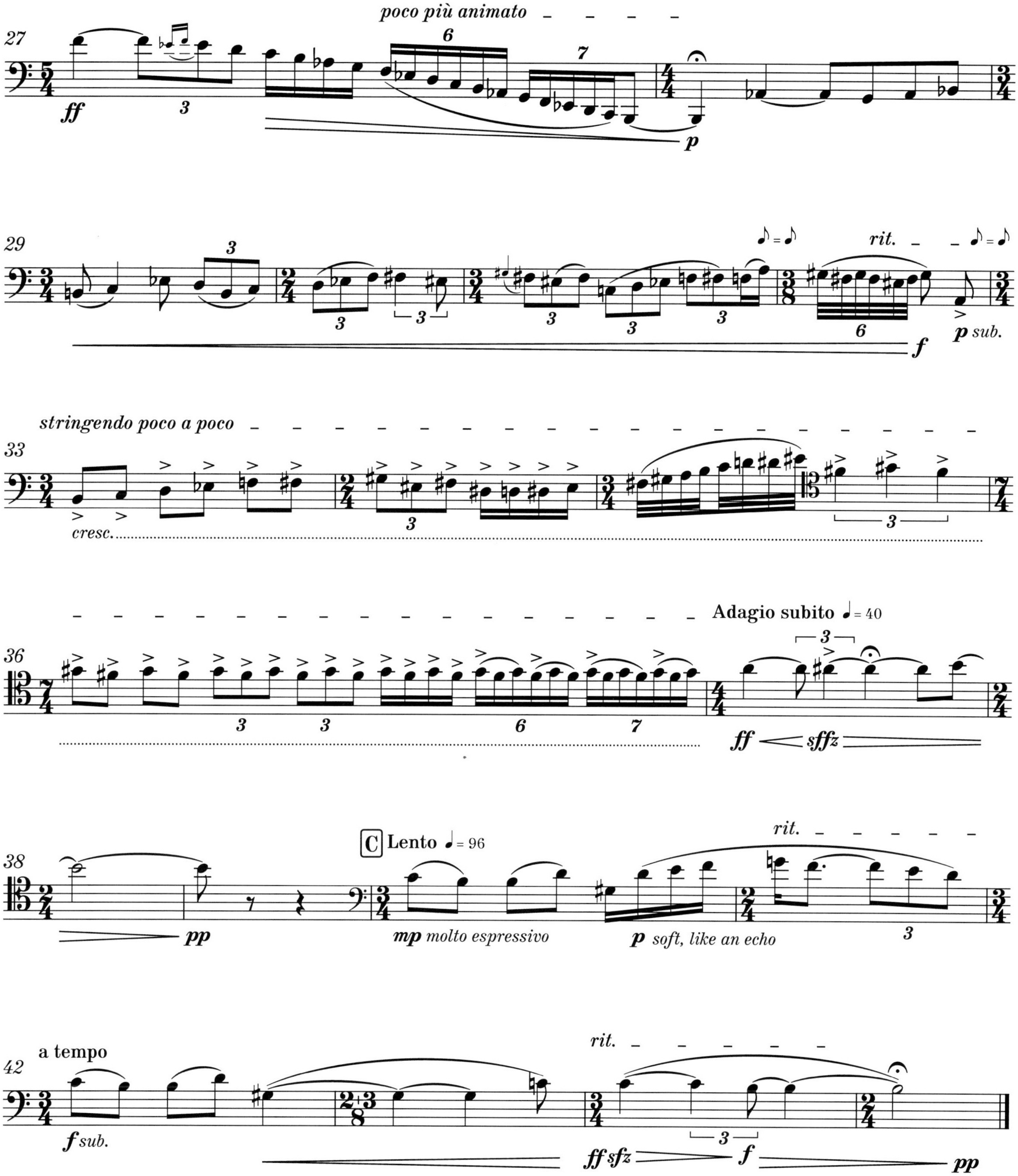
poco più animato
ff
p
rit.
f
p sub.
stringendo poco a poco
cresc.
Adagio subito ♩= 40
ff
sffz
C
Lento ♩= 96
pp
mp molto espressivo
p soft, like an echo
rit.
a tempo
f sub.
rit.
ff sfz
f
pp

II.

D
Lento ♩. = 72
Pno
Meno mosso ♩. = 60
f
4
6
9
11
ff
14
16
rit.
a tempo
E
f
20
22
mf
f

F
poco sostenuto
a tempo
rit.
G
Più mosso ♩. = 96
G.P.
Adagio ♩ = 40
rit.
Più mosso ♩ = 92
Meno mosso ♩ = 82
rit.
Meno mosso ♩ = 69
rit.
♩=56
♩=42
Largo ♪ = 50
Meno mosso ♪ = 44

Page intentionally left blank to facilitate page turn

III.

H Adagio ♩= 42
Bassoon
Piano
cue
p
l.v.
mp
Ped. sempre (leave the sustaining pedal down throughout this movement)
6
mf molto espressivo e cantabile
pp sub.
9
ppp

12
mf
l.v.
15
start slowly and gradually speed up
I
rit.
a tempo
f
mp
18
poco sost.
a tempo
20
♩ = ♩. (♩. = 42)
mf
23
♩. = ♩ (♩ = 42)
15ma
ppp

*) Stay motionless for five seconds, then attacca to the next movement.

IV.

K
Allegro scherzando ♩ = 138
ca. 3"
Pno
with flair and "schmaltz" like a folk musician
f espr.
mf cresc.
poco rit.
a tempo
poco rit.
a tempo
rit.
L
a tempo

37
ff sfz
sfz sfz
40
M
mf cresc.
43
48
ff sfz
ff
50
sfz pp
ff
sfz
F♯ multiphonic
(underblow)
sfz
ca. 2"
Molto meno mosso ♩= 69
sfz pp sub.
rit. molto rit.
Subito più mosso ♩= 126
55
ff
pp
fff
molto rit.
ffff sfz sfz
sfz

V.

N
Andante ♩. = 58
mf molto espressivo
♪ = ♪
6
12
rit.
O
Poco più animato ♩. = 66
p
f sub.
17
sostenuto
Meno mosso ♩. = 50
rit. poco a poco
♩. = ♩ (♩=50)
22
Molto meno mosso ♩ = 44
rit.
P
Poco meno mosso ♩ = 56
Tempo I
mp
mf
p
p sotto voce
27
sostenuto
rit.
Meno mosso ♩. = 44
poco rit.
poco fp
pp

VI.

Q
Allegro scherzando ♩. = 126
Pno
mf leggiero
6
mf
11
rit.
Poco meno mosso ♩. = 120
f
17
molto rit.

R
Molto meno mosso ♩. = 50
poco sost.
a tempo
sostenuto
f molto espressivo
ff
molto rit.
più molto rit.
Adagio ♩ = 48
Poco più mosso ♩ = 50
mp
rit.
stringendo poco a poco
p
pp
sfz
f
S
Tempo I
Allegro scherzando ♩. = 126
mf leggiero
mf
ossia
molto rit.
7:4
Tempo I ♩. = 126
dim.
T
pp
rit.
Meno mosso ♩ = 60
rit.
attacca

Acknowledgements from the Arranger

I would like to extend my sincerest thanks to

Reza Vali,
for your beautiful music as well as your willingness to collaborate and support making it accessible for bassoonists.

Ronald Krentzman,
for your essential copyist contributions and for creating the newly engraved edition.

Rémy Taghavi,
for collaborating with me on this project and bringing attention to the practical aspects of bassoon performance.

Janna Baty,
for providing me with the texts and translations to the original set, *The Being of Love*.

Yale School of Music,
for giving me the opportunity to present and premiere this music on stage in Morse Recital Hall, Sprague Memorial Hall at Yale University in March 2025.

Sandro Alexander Tsereteli,
for your exceptional talents as a pianist and your dear friendship.

Frank Morelli,
for the outstanding guidance you have given to my studies, the artistic insights with which you have musically empowered me, and the care and to which you have encouraged my growth.

My Grandmother,
who, at the age of 90, has looked after me throughout my journey, and for whom I dedicate much of my professional work.

My Parents,
for unconditionally loving my ideas, my idiosyncrasies, and my innocence.

VII.

U
Molto allegro ♩ = 132
poco sost.
Poco meno mosso ♩ = 120–126
V
molto espressivo e cantabile
pp sub.
f sub.
W

*) This may be played one octave lower through measure 58.

Z Più mosso (Tempo I) ♩= 132
AA Meno mosso ♩= 126
cresc.
p sub.
cresc. poco a poco
Più mosso ♩= 144
BB
bisbigliando
RH
B♭
G
A♭
sempre simile
fff sub.
ppp sub.
CC Meno mosso ♩= 120
rit.
molto rit.
Meno mosso ♩= 96